THE COST OF WALKING

THE COST OF WALKING

Poems by

Shannon Tharp

SKYSILL PRESS

MMXI

ISBN 978-1-907489-06-8

Cover painting: "Open Up", 30"x24", 2009 by Gary Petersen
Copyright © Gary Petersen
Private collection
Photo courtesy Jason Mandella

SKYSILL PRESS
3 Gervase Gardens
Clifton Village
Nottingham   NG11 8LZ

skysillpress.blogspot.com

CONTENTS

ACKNOWLEDGEMENTS

Previous versions of these poems were published in the following journals: *Asterisk, BPM, Cranky Literary Journal, The Cultural Society, Dusie, Effing Magazine, Free Verse: A Journal of Contemporary Poetry & Poetics, MARY, /nor: The New Ohio Review, The New Yinzer, Shampoo, Sixth Finch,* & *Wandering Army.* Many thanks to their editors.

Thanks also to Mandy Olson, who published several of these poems in an Elliott Press chapbook (*Each Real Bird*), to Jess Mynes, who published several more of them in a Fewer & Further Press chapbook (*Determined by Aperture*) and to Alisa Heinzman and Sara Mumolo who are publishing even more of them in a Calaveras chapbook (*Quarry*).

Thanks to Gary Petersen for the use of "Open Up".

To Zach Barocas, Nicole Burgund, Paul Ebenkamp, Graham Foust, Maggie Jackson, Joseph Massey, Heather McHugh, and John Taggart: something beyond thanks (and words) to you for your thoughtfulness and generosity at critical junctures in this writing's growth.

And for everything, love to Christine, Janet and Terry Tharp.

Better the wind, the sea, the salt
in your eyes,
than this, this, this.

H. D.

DUSK

The chime of an ice cream truck
materializes. A moth ticks obliquely
against a darkening screen.

> *(This could be any world.*
> *This could be any nerve.*

This
is the crucially useless circus
in which I rehearse the bruise
I miss you.

> *There will always be*
> *a hand beyond*
> *weather—*

fire's immediacy
sharpest in frost.

WINDCHILL

A change
       in the weather
is known to be extreme.

What it is not
       is managed
              or imagined.

       Loss is loss is loss

       repeated. And
breathing stings
       below zero.

BIRTHDAY

Nearly unfailing
you say Here's
your snow.

The world could show
nothing
to me,

arterial ends
good and
red.

I happen
to be an accident
your hand recorded in a tunnel.

POEM

Graphic
    as a flower
  blooms
a split lark's
  minor
    stream.

FROM A MOTHER

Discomfort
is a cut

that doesn't
close, dove.

Your birthday
occurs

every time
you turn

around.

WAKING

There is nothing
to turn from
or to.

I hardly
see at all.

All I remember
I remember
in pieces,

as when
shadows

lapse into
shadows
when

bars of light
flood a wall.

WITHIN REASON

Woke voiceless, wanting
to sing in the city
where people say rain
spells weather, where
one goes gray with
waiting. I used to think
to find my way around;
now I go braving
anything that I can't
think to see. Things
go luminous (within
reason) without light.

NEBRASKA

A caravan's mapless dirge
sulks into windmills'
listless terror
of trees.

•

I'll turn the key,
quarry my worry to sleep
under intricate bridges. All it takes
is you taking my hand.

•

The horizon's plum bloomed
a colored dozen of the same kind
and I can't stop thinking my sight: if it were a city,
I'd punch its lights out.

•

Sad monuments, these reminders—
guns, paper, and tires—
are what you are. The string
I never tied around my finger.

•

Few places are beautiful
in the dark, and you're the first.
I don't need light
to learn why.

•

My heart
in a hazard of cars
moves closer to knowing
you're nothing I can cry for, to.

THE WHOLE SCENE COMES BEFORE US

1

Stars: just
stars.

Traffic:
facts.

Close
your eyes.

It's bright
enough.

2

We point
to locate.

That is,
there is

responsibility
in vision.

3

Lost things go
somewhere.

Our place
is belated.

ORCHARD

A god-
thought

field
where

even
rain

loses
heart

when
shadows'

shadows
fall

as they
ought.

YOU ARE ONLY HALF OF YOU

One thinks
where one spoke—

a viable
site, like a

platform—a church
determined

by aperture.
Shadows

register
a room.

Trees repeat
a door.

•

Barn-dark,
night-far,

a gift's
the drowse you burn in.

Someone comes through

the hall
like weather.

A map's in
the wheels of

her drawl.

PRACTICE

for Jack Spicer

Down
every road
there's always
one more system—
some cruelly intricate
winter between
issue and
return.

Snow
appears
in settings

where
nothing's
being built.

You lose the
radio in a
basin
and

listen
to decay.

Monday, fact.
Tuesday, fact.

A needle, a nettle, a wind.

There hasn't been an accident since
birds were disturbed
into sitting.

The landscape's a field
inundated with geese.

You say places you
remember from
maps.

As if,
in reciprocity,
something sees you
saying, progressive arcs unfold.

Given your heart's ardor,
a field is not a choice.

To record
more convincingly
the force behind motion,
you'll walk through
a posture of
nerves.

STEADY, LESS AND LESS

The day flickers before us in a thicked-up throb
of questions. What of birds and the peculiarity of
flight—a pattern by which to scratch

existence. What of me and the inexpense of
sitting in a field with your face
to any nameable thing.

When simply the having is enough
will you ask, "How are you
breathing, my girl?"

IF WE MAKE IT THROUGH DECEMBER

Vessels
drift.

Letters
alight.

In the hemlock,
I pale,

unpacked
as a foal.

Were snow
to animate

the smallest
gray creature—

give it legs
and plot—

I would
think

to turn
to you, and

in returning,
arc.

VITAL SIGNS

Sister,
don't reduce
yourself. Somewhere
rooms share a pattern.
There are thoughts
there, large
as air.

There are
masses of bright
flowers. And how is it far
if we think it. What
is it that we
know.

The
bitter ease
of profit, simple
terror of the
sea.

A little
flesh, a little
breath in preparation
for a dream. Frame
of bone pulled
hollow,

I wish
what I wished
you before. There's
not a bird in the world
worth your undying hurt
and I can't undo
the future.

POEM WITHOUT DOOR

There's a bird sounds like
a hinge in
the early morning,

a transmission turn-
ing over
and over to fail

as the sun proceeds
to rightly
cut into the room

in which paint and its
gradations
level our waking.

MORNING (WITH WILLIAM BRONK)

The world, what we took
for the world,
is breaking. *Breaking!*

•

Your point: night's over.
And we are
equally alive.

BLUE COLLAR COMEDY

A whistle
is hit

in a dance.
A rabbit

in a rigged
pit

hobbles,
conscious

of a flawed hop.
Cattle as soggy

props needle
into green.

Blasted clear
and shattered,

the skin's
nation's

a slow notion
of marrow,

pulse
just

that.
All we ask

is that
you make us laugh.

We've plenty
of contempt

for the
genuine.

THE MISFITS

For breaking's
sake, be far
away.

*—you know
corrosion*

*grates
shapes.)*

As in
Christmas cards to which
we'll never reply, to which
scissors fit in

half
light.

NORTHERLY

In conditions less
than perfect,
what I make out through

rain—happening a-
gain in a
slow diagonal—

white hearse, green graveyard,
little else
save for what isn't.

PAPER

Not yet
rained
on, all
you say
brings
to mind
a rock.

CHASING LANDMARKS

Near the harbor: cars—
a succession of glassed-
in heads. I stare
at an undercarriage
(Tennessee semi)
and hoard my
disorders.

2

How
to make out the cloud-

accurate
mountain

through mid-afternoon
gridlock.

•

"There's a door—
        that's the point here—
                if you want some time to yourself."

                The speed limit removes
        what few songs
I knew.

•

An ambulance
drives

against
traffic

somewhere
between

Graveyard and
Stadium.

3

Grid
of lights,

lit
for night. Wet

leaves—
tarps—

drape
a house.

4

For days
the same
trucks—

too much
construction.
Today

I could
not fall
in love.

5

In the patient laying out of
this endurable fracture
a kite only appears to go up.

Red numbers
above the moon
on the floor,

hoarse
with how
long I've known

you.

Evasion's an angel's
legacy.
I look

at alarm
as
a

wife.

6

a hug   from my mother
a fist fight   with a stranger
filthy, difficult   sex

homemade ghost—
sibilant
par-

        a-

           chute—
           spinning
           in the wind

harbor seals bark
      across
        fog

           to
           my feet
           sediment adheres

7

The
world—
your world—

rounding
a cor-
ner:

sun
on a truck
full of shovels.

8

Autonomy
     dismantles valleys

here
where it's windowless.

Remnants
     —nets—
commemorate

       a world.

     Naked,

awake,

      (I think).

9

When we
revisit

intricate
bridges

you speak
of a barge

struggling
at night,

a hospital's
indifference

to rain. This
has taken

years, this
admitting—

the cost
of walking

crying
alike.

10

Unintended
island,
cut

from what
forests
absorb.

Oars
adjust
to substance,

the rhythm: *not
yours*. Not
yours.

COMMUTE

Rain on
the lake, its
barrels of
paint; a few
leaves move
in circles
on the
surface.

A song
borrowed
until useless
is a new vacancy
felt—cars and
all, cars and
all—in the
same place
you wake
to day
after day.

And said
music, its
room, turns
from thought
to water to
words—my
love, you're
doing fine,
you're on TV—
to birds on the
periphery
where
an oil rig
floats in fog.

SERIAL

Pain
akin to a
waveless lake—
palpable and blue—
this headache's the episode
in which I return
to myself
unused.

RESIDUAL

Almost
turned

into
an orchard

before
you remembered

not to
breathe.

Better
to be

a lost
ball

in high
grass

than
an irrepressible stretch

of trees.

CALIFORNIA

elk

left
to make do with

stems

TRAVELOGUE

Gulls at low tide,
unconcernedly
quiet.

Weather's
the only
explanation.

•

Driven
   inland

   (downpour's
approach)

we cross
   yellow roses

   thriving
among

dull
brush.

•

Stalled here,
we argue.

Our words
dislodge
fog.

•

Obdurate
waver,

my late
portrait,

take
your eyes

made of
a world

I don't
know

what
to make of.

•

The
ocean

reasserts
itself.

Each
wave

makes
a crater.

POEM

occupant-starved
margin

bent

on whoever
you are

GOLDEN GARDENS PARK

A train
goes by and

small
waves

raise
torn

sails—some
daughter's

identical
clatter

the ocean
lowered

into
cold.

IMPALPABLE

One's
   need
these
   closed-
in days
   to say
the sky's
   diluted
by clouds.

DRAIN

an eyelash in
an otherwise white sink

A BASIC APPROACH TO THE FACE

Headfirst
into a field sketch,

the mouth is capable
of accepting every
shade.

Make
a picture.

Try to see
the sun.

It's fine.

You'll never
look at me from
where I am.

ALLERGY

Just because I feel disease
doesn't mean
it's mine.

*(Altitude
flinches.*

*An apple
splits.)*

By way of highest pollen,
this flower-pain
is yours.

AFTER ASTRONOMY

Straining for a picture, I remember
your face—the winter I said
I'd never describe.

This lie remains
provokingly stable, vacant
not with space, but with pain.

And it's ruthless that it comes as no surprise,
freezing news, ruin, you, or whoever
I confess to the dark.

Going back over
what was done, there
is almost not an interval.

Apples fall without astronomy,
thus I fall asleep
with a gun.

Thus a room's
kissed away in radiance;
nothing's left to be touched.

Books, porcelain, windows are open,
and heaven could be said
to be a wreck.

The clouds are here,
they aren't up in the sky—that's
your handwriting, that's the way you write.

I told you I need something
to hold—here I am cold
with you, without.

STATE LINE

A hasty graveyard's makeshift
fence, boarded houses and
token snow, stained pavement
where a carcass bled, covered horses
with no place to go, an old barn
slowly collapsing between refineries
and grains, a rare bridge among infinite
hills, and one last bird (and another) through
your brain, stalled boxcars and broken
jukeboxes, a field cut within an inch
of its dirt—like so—railroad
parallel singed crops, and
wind winding across the highway
with the look of dry ice
in a place no worse than your earth.

TO EARTH

No way
into your face,

just a flame to be
at home in,

and so I come
to understand

cold. Far away
slowly, shapes

take the place
of snow, until

even weather
appears to be

dead. What late
thought, what

careful error—
that hearing in you

spares me.

PROOF

Time leaves us words, love,
old things to
which we return, so

there are new leaves, new
dead leaves, to-
gether in the dirt.

WAKING BEFORE ALARM

I look
away from
air turning
where sun fuses
with dust.

Buntings
I mistook
for new leaves
up and empty
the tree.

HIGH RISE

Illiterate
here,

sequestered
there,

those
windows

are just
a house

torn around
auroras

we know
as distortions.

Evenly
spaced
vehicles
press into
a flock of hail.

Anger's
made stranger
by self-editing.

To forgive you
each day's
a ritual.

There,
where

least
words

thaw
taut water,

everything
wants a narrative.

One copes with
helicopters

by choosing
a bird

to listen
to.

Crow
towing
a sliver
of tinsel—Again—
its color
drew
you.

Night
clouds a violet's
inversion.

Suddenly
the sun's
a stone.

Mirror,
improbable as
when you first saw

it. You own it.
You own it
now.

CONCEDED

for John Taggart

How
to love
quietly

what
wasn't
seen before—

leaves
or trees,
their shadows,

what
did I know,
what did I know—

to be
woken by
a memory

of
something
one thought gone,

which
is what
is wanted,

which is
a song.

GRAND CANYON

From space, a ragged
scar. Someone's

named it beautiful—
Most Beautiful—

and its history's clear,
though the picture's

distant. Five hundred
miles away, the moon

is a hatchet of silver,
prepared to slip into

whatever earth needs
cutting. Five hundred

miles away, the stars
are locked in dark, are

breaking with us as
we sleep, breathe, or

can't. You're in my
heart; I'm in your

hand. This world—
glass upon inversion—

is a mirror in which
greater figures exist,

in which, waiting,
they remain.

AN EDGE

Patience now's
a more substantive

shadow, as in
waves changing

in the dark.
There's an echo

here, the ghost of
which is something

like a voice that grows
as it's eroded. What

remains is listening's
trace, a struggle

for another pattern;
a growing into

need, want;
a process to not

remember. One
learns this ground

through
flashes of doubt.

www.ingramcontent.com/pod-product-compliance
Lightning Source LLC
Chambersburg PA
CBHW020949090426
42736CB00010B/1340